the simple
SALVATION
BIBLE STUDY

the simple SALVATION
BIBLE STUDY

W. TAYLOR FISH

The Simple Salvation Bible Study

Published by Truth Book Company, LLC
Anderson, IN

ISBN 979-8-9895526-6-5, paperback

Cover Design: Liz Fulgencio Davis

We hope you enjoy this book from Truth Book Company.
Our goal is to provide high-quality, Bible-based books,
curriculum, and resources to equip you to stand for
truth. For more information on our other books and
resources, please visit **www.truthbook.co.**

To place a wholesale order of *The Simple Salvation
Bible Study*, contact us at: **wholesale@truthbook.co**

A MESSAGE TO THE TEACHER

In my early years of soul winning, I remember flipping through my Bible and watching the eyes of my student light up as scripture began to bring them real revelation. At that time I didn't teach proven bible studies written by someone else. I would just read scripture and explain it from my Bible. I won't say that this was always the best method, it wasn't scripted, and I did find myself at some dead ends with more biblically educated students. Even so, teaching directly from my Bible did teach me a powerful lesson. The Word works.

Something powerful happens when the Word of God is delivered to another through a Bible study. The Word enters the eyes and the ears, and it journeys to the heart. As the Word is taught it will tear down great walls, erase old lies, and reveal hidden truths. The Word will do what we cannot do if we will just teach it.

In my travels I am often approached by burdened Apostolics who want tips on teaching their first Bible study. Too many are intimidated by the thought of the process of teaching a Bible study. It is very easy to overthink teaching a Bible study. Understand as you hold this Bible study in your hands that you do not have to be intimidated or overthink it anymore. The outline has already been created for you, and the Word will work as it is vocalized. If you can read it, you can teach it. It really is that simple. I usually ask my student to read the scriptures out loud, and then I will teach the rest of the Bible study to them reading it exactly as it is written.

I taught this exact same Bible study to a gang member in California, a witch in Wisconsin, a cocaine addict in Texas, and a seasoned denominal preacher in Kentucky. They were all baptized in the name of Jesus Christ afterward. There are many great stories of victory that have come through this tool. I have taught this at kitchen tables, in living rooms, in coffee shops, in restaurants, over ZOOM, and the list goes on. Much of the content here I preached in a field at the Asbury revival in Willmore, Kentucky early in 2023. We saw many filled with the Holy Ghost that day, and others were baptized in the name of Jesus Christ as a result. I tell you this because I want you to know that this outline has been both tweaked and proven many times, and that you can be confident teaching this, even as a first time Bible study teacher. This Bible study is geared for conversions, and it is very simple to teach.

Now I challenge you to find a student. Don't just wait for an opportunity, but find one. Make that call. Send that text. Have that conversation. Tell somebody that you have a powerful 30 minute Bible study that you would like to teach them. Offer to buy lunch, coffee, or ice cream. Do whatever it takes to get a student. After teaching this Bible study, stick with your student and plug them in to an extended weekly Bible study. It's time for you to win a soul!

"Go ye therefore, and teach…" (Matthew 28:19 KJV)

- Evg. Taylor Fish

Follow Taylor Fish
on Instagram
@revtaylorfish

SALVATION
BIBLE STUDY

JOHN 3:16 (KJV)

> *16 For God so loved the world, that he gave his only begotten Son, that whosoever believeth in him should not perish, but have everlasting life.*

Across many different faiths and denominations, this is the most memorized scripture in all of the Bible. Most likely we have all seen John 3:16 displayed on clothing, vehicles, and billboards. Though this scripture displays the greatest love ever known to man, this scripture is too often misinterpreted.

1 TIMOTHY 3:16 (KJV)

> *16 And without controversy great is the mystery of godliness: God was manifest in the flesh, justified in the Spirit, seen of angels, preached unto the Gentiles, believed on in the world, received up into glory.*

Like John 3:16, this verse shows us that God became a man, known as Jesus Christ, to die for us. It also says that people in the world believed on him. They were believers.

BELIEVING THAT JESUS IS OUR GOD AND OUR PERSONAL SAVIOR IS VERY IMPORTANT, BUT IS THIS ALL IT TAKES TO BE SAVED?

1

JAMES 2:14, 19-20 (KJV)

14 What doth it profit, my brethren, though a man say he hath faith, and have not works? can faith save him?

19 Thou believest that there is one God; thou doest well: the devils also believe, and tremble.

20 But wilt thou know, O vain man, that faith without works is dead?

The definition of faith is something that is believed especially with strong conviction.

James asked the question: *"can faith* (or can faith alone) *save"* us? He then answered his question by saying *"faith without works is dead."* James tells us that having faith in God, or believing in him or on him, is not enough. True faith will lead us to works. True faith will cause us to take steps in obedience to God's Holy Word.

Here, James tells us that the devils also believe in the one true God. In Mark 1:24, devils called Jesus *"the Holy One."* The devils proved that they believed and knew who Jesus was. This is another fact that proves that faith alone cannot save. Even though devils believe that Jesus Christ is the one true God and savior, they will never be saved. Believing alone is not enough!

2 TIMOTHY 3:16-17 (KJV)

16 All scripture is given by inspiration of God, and is profitable for doctrine, for reproof, for correction, for instruction in righteousness:

17 That the man of God may be perfect, thoroughly furnished unto all good works.

2

Here, Paul shows us that God's plan for salvation is not found in one scripture alone, but it is found in all scripture. All scripture was given to us by God through men to show us the way. When we take the whole Bible we will find doctrine, reproof, correction, and instruction. We must obey all scripture, not just bits and pieces of it.

God's Word directs us *"unto all good works,"* and obedience to that direction *"perfects us."*

THE FULL STORY: YOU MUST BE BORN AGAIN

One thing that is very important to understand is that John 3:16, our opening scripture, is one verse in a 21 verse conversation that started in John 3:1. It is a powerful verse, but one scripture is not all scripture.

HAVE YOU EVER HAD SOMEONE REPEAT ONLY A PORTION OF YOUR CONVERSATION?

There are few things more frustrating than this because when this happens it keeps the listener from hearing the full story and knowing the speaker's full meaning. This is exactly the case here in John 3. Many put so much emphasis on John 3:16 that they miss what Jesus made plain. Let's back up and see the full story.

JOHN 3:3-5, 7 (KJV)

> *3 Jesus answered and said unto him, Verily, verily, I say unto thee, Except a man be born again, he cannot **see** the kingdom of God.*

4 Nicodemus saith unto him, How can a man be born when he is old? can he enter the second time into his mother's womb, and be born?

*5 Jesus answered, Verily, verily, I say unto thee, <u>Except a man be born of water and of the Spirit, he cannot **enter** into the kingdom of God.</u>*

7 Marvel not that I said unto thee, Ye <u>must</u> be born again.

We just read a very big *"must"* in Scripture. A must is not optional. Jesus said *"Marvel not,"* or don't be surprised that I'm telling you that you must be born again.

Believing that Jesus is the one true God and our personal savior is very important, but it is also important that we do not skip through the beginning of the chapter and fail to see all that Jesus was telling Nicodemus. Jesus said that if a person is not born again of water and of the Spirit, then that person cannot see or enter into the kingdom of God.

Jesus spoke of a powerful spiritual experience that allowed us to see the kingdom and enter into it!

To believe, but not be born again, does not fulfill the commandments of Jesus.

True faith will lead us to obey the words of Jesus. This is how we see and enter the kingdom of God. Jesus spoke of both a water birth, and a Spirit birth. You and I MUST be born again of both WATER AND SPIRIT! Let's take a look at what it means to be born of both water and Spirit.

THREE ACCOUNTS OF THE SAME STORY

In the New Testament, the books of Matthew, Mark, Luke, and John are known as the four gospels of Jesus Christ. These were men who wrote the story of Jesus from their perspective.

If we were asked to write a police report as witnesses of a car accident that we saw, chances are that our stories would read differently, but there would be many similarities and common denominators. Here we will see 3 different accounts of the same story as Jesus spoke of the water and Spirit birth.

MATTHEW 28:18-20 (KJV)

> *18 And Jesus came and spake unto them, saying, All power is given unto me in heaven and in earth.*
>
> *19 Go ye therefore, and teach all nations, baptizing them in the name of the Father, and of the Son, and of the Holy Ghost:*
>
> *20 Teaching them to observe all things whatsoever I have commanded you: and, lo, I am with you always, even unto the end of the world. Amen.*

In Matthew's account, Jesus tells his disciples to go, teach, and baptize in the name of the Father, and of the Son, and of the Holy Ghost, and then to teach again! Teaching was very important here. Teaching was so important that Jesus commanded them to teach before and after baptism.

The main reason that much of the religious world baptizes using the titles, Father, Son, and Holy Ghost, is because there is a great lack of teaching. It is also important to note that there was never a baptismal service in Scripture where someone was baptized using these titles.

BAPTISM IS THE WATER BIRTH, and must be done correctly *"in the name."*

We must understand that Father is not a name, Son is not a name, and neither is Holy Ghost. They are simply titles, and not names. Let's see the second account of the same story.

MARK 16:15-17 (KJV)

> *15 And he said unto them, Go ye into all the world, and preach the gospel to every creature.*
>
> *16 He that believeth and is baptized shall be saved; but he that believeth not shall be damned.*
>
> *17 And these signs shall follow them that believe; In my name shall they cast out devils; they shall speak with new tongues;*

In Mark's account we see that baptism is not just a good deed, but that it is essential for salvation. Again, baptism is the water birth! In verse 17, we see Jesus uses the phrase *"in my name."*

Jesus also speaks of the Spirit birth when he speaks of the signs that will follow believers. He says, *"they shall speak with new tongues."*

LUKE 24:45-49 (KJV)

> *45 Then opened he their understanding, that they might understand the scriptures,*

46 And said unto them, Thus it is written, and thus it behooved Christ to suffer, and to rise from the dead the third day:

47 <u>And that repentance and remission of sins should be preached in his name</u> among all nations, beginning at Jerusalem.

It is important to note that Jesus opened their understanding.

At this point these disciples had walked with Jesus for years, they had witnessed the miracles, and they had heard His teaching. They were true believers. Saying that, there came a day where Jesus opened up their understanding to more. We must always be willing to let the word of God show us something new.

Here, in Luke's account, Jesus spoke of repentance. Repentance is when we confess, ask for forgiveness, and turn away from our sins. Repentance is our choice to change. Repentance is what we do.

Then Jesus speaks of *"remission of sins."* If someone was to have cancer, and the doctor said "your cancer has gone into remission", then that would mean that their cancer was no more. The remitting, or the washing away of sin from someone's life only comes through baptism in the name.

Here is our conclusion. Matthew wrote *"in the name,"* Mark wrote *"in my name,"* and Luke wrote *"in his name."* This is no coincidence. The name was mentioned in every instance, because it is the name that makes the difference! Baptism must be done in the name of Jesus Christ.

Let's continue in this story. Jesus goes on to say:

48 And ye are witnesses of these things.

49 And, behold, I send the promise of my Father upon you: but tarry ye in the city of Jerusalem, until ye be endued with power from on high.

Jesus said He was sending something powerful to Jerusalem. Many did not obey the words of Jesus and chose not to go to Jerusalem, but others did. Let's go to Jerusalem and see what happens!

A PROMISE IN JERUSALEM

ACTS 2:1-4 (KJV)

1 And when the day of Pentecost was fully come, they were all with one accord in one place.

2 And suddenly there came a sound from heaven as of a rushing mighty wind, and it filled all the house where they were sitting.

3 And there appeared unto them cloven tongues like as of fire, and it sat upon each of them.

4 And they were all filled with the Holy Ghost, and began to speak with other tongues, as the Spirit gave them utterance.

Verse 3 shows us that after 10 days of prayer in the upper room, heaven came to earth. What was taking place was from heaven. This was the promise that Jesus had spoken about earlier in Luke 24:49.

What happened inside that upper prayer room was not a normal moment, but it was a heavenly moment. It was misunderstood by those outside of the room, but undeniably real to those who were in the room.

They were *"all filled with the Holy Ghost"* and began to speak in a heavenly language. This is the 1st account of people being born of the Spirit, and every person in the room spoke with tongues that they had never spoken before.

Speaking in tongues is God's plan for every New Testament believer. Remember, Jesus said in Mark 16:17 *"they shall speak with new tongues."* Shall is a promise. Jesus was saying that believers shall be tongue talkers.

WHY DID GOD CHOOSE THE TONGUE?

James 3:8 (KJV)

> 8 But the tongue can no man tame; it is an unruly evil, full of deadly poison.

Inside the tongue lies man's greatest weakness. Relationships are destroyed because of things that were said. People are hurt because of the tongue. The tongue lies. The tongue gossips. The tongue attacks. There are people in the grave today because of things that were said. James said that the tongue is *"unruly evil."*

It must also be said that inside the tongue lies man's greatest strength and power. God chose speaking in tongues as the initial sign of filling a person with the baptism of the Holy Ghost. Speaking in tongues is the ultimate sign of surrender. God knew that if he could have a man's unruly tongue, that he could fill him with power and use that man for his glory.

When someone receives the Holy Ghost there will be many signs, gifts, and fruits that are displayed in their life throughout their walk with God, but they will first speak with tongues. This is a Bible experience for us all.

It is important to note that this supernatural experience happened after a lingering time of prayer and pursuit towards God. If you are hungry for this experience, you must go after it with repentance, prayer, praise, faith, and persistence. Get vocal. Seek the Lord with your whole heart and heaven will come to you. As you seek God, you will soon feel the Spirit moving on your lips, and then you will speak with heavenly tongues just as they did in the book of Acts.

PETER PREACHES
THE WATER & SPIRIT BIRTH
IN JERUSALEM

ACTS 2:36-41 (KJV)

36 Therefore let all the house of Israel know assuredly, that God hath made the same Jesus, whom ye have crucified, both Lord and Christ.

Here, Simon Peter preaches to the Jews that they had crucified the one true God, Jesus Christ.

37 Now when they heard this, <u>they were pricked in their heart</u>, and said unto Peter and to the rest of the apostles, Men and brethren, <u>what shall we do?</u>

After hearing this, the Jews were *"pricked in their heart."* It was a feeling of conviction. We all know what it feels like when God begins to pull at our heart.

This pricking of the heart led to a question, and this is still being asked today. They asked, *"What shall we do?"* or

"What shall we do to be saved?" Peter answers their question in the next verse.

> *38 Then Peter said unto them, <u>Repent,</u> and be baptized every one of you in the name of Jesus Christ <u>for the remission of sins,</u> and <u>ye shall receive the gift of the Holy Ghost.</u>*
>
> *39 For the <u>promise</u> is unto you, and to your children, and to all that are afar off, even as many as the Lord our God shall call.*
>
> *40 And with many other words did he testify and exhort, saying, <u>Save yourselves</u> from this untoward generation.*
>
> *41 <u>Then they that gladly received his word were baptized:</u> and the same day there were added unto them about three thousand souls.*

Peter preached repentance (which is the commitment to turn from sin), baptism in the name of Jesus Christ (which is the water birth), and the infilling of the Holy Ghost (which is the Spirit birth)!

Remember, this passage of Scripture takes place in Jerusalem, and this was the fulfillment of the words of Jesus in Luke 24:47 when He said, *<u>"repentance and remission of sins should be preached in his name</u> among all nations, beginning at Jerusalem."*

3000 people had their sins remitted by being baptized in the name of Jesus Christ that day. Baptism in the name of Jesus Christ is the only way that you and I can have a clean slate.

ACTS 19:1-6 (KJV)

1 And it came to pass, that, while Apollos was at Corinth, Paul having passed through the upper coasts came to Ephesus: and finding certain disciples,

2 He said unto them, <u>Have ye received the Holy Ghost since ye believed?</u> And they said unto him, We have not so much as heard whether there be any Holy Ghost.

3 And he said unto them, <u>Unto what then were ye baptized?</u> And they said, Unto John's baptism.

4 Then said Paul, John verily baptized with the baptism of repentance, saying unto the people, that they should believe on him which should come after him, that is, on Christ Jesus.

5 <u>When they heard this, they were baptized in the name of the Lord Jesus.</u>

6 And when Paul had laid his hands upon them, <u>the Holy Ghost came on them; and they spake with tongues,</u> and prophesied.

The disciples of John were believers in Jesus Christ, but had not heard of the new birth message. They did not know what the Holy Ghost was.

They had also been baptized before, but were re-baptized when they realized that they had not been baptized in the name of the Lord Jesus Christ.

They were re-baptized by the Apostle Paul. When they came out of the water, they received the baptism of the Holy Ghost/Spirit with the evidence of speaking in tongues! This is another great example of both the water birth and the Spirit birth in the same instance.

Paul preached the water and Spirit message there in Ephesus, but this would not be his last encounter with Ephesus.

EPHESIANS 4:5 (KJV)

5 One Lord, one faith, one baptism,

Just as Paul preached in Ephesus to the disciples of John, he also wrote to Ephesus here in the book of Ephesians saying that there is *"one Lord,"* who we know as Jesus, there is *"one faith,"* or one way to believe, and there is also *"one baptism,"* or one way to be baptized!

That one way to be baptized is the same way they were baptized throughout the book of Acts. Acts chapters 2, 8, 10, 19, and 22 all have examples of people being baptized in the name of Jesus Christ. Again, there is not one biblical reference anywhere in the Scripture of people being baptized under the titles Father, Son, and Holy Ghost.

Baptism in the name of Jesus Christ is the *"one baptism"* water birth that Paul was writing about!

PAUL WRITES TO THOSE WHO WERE ALREADY BORN AGAIN OF BOTH WATER & SPIRIT

1 CORINTHIANS 6:9-11 (KJV)

9 Know ye not that the unrighteous shall not inherit the kingdom of God? Be not deceived: neither fornicators, nor idolaters, nor adulterers, nor effeminate, nor abusers of themselves with mankind,

10 Nor thieves, nor covetous, nor drunkards, nor revilers, nor extortioners, shall inherit the kingdom of God.

11 <u>And such were some of you: but ye are washed, but ye are sanctified, but ye are justified in the name of the Lord Jesus, and by the Spirit of our God.</u>

Paul spoke of the sinners that would not enter the kingdom God. He then told the church at Corinth, *"and such WERE some of you."* This is a very important statement. Paul was recognizing the fact that though there was a time that they were sinners like this, they were not who they used to be, because they had been baptized in the name of the Lord Jesus Christ, and filled with His Spirit!

It is very clear. We are washed, sanctified, and justified one way and one way alone. That is by repenting of our sins, being baptized in the name of the Lord Jesus Christ, and by receiving the Spirit of God with the evidence of speaking in tongues.

TWO VERY IMPORTANT QUESTIONS:

1. CAN WE REPENT TOGETHER?

Remember this is confessing, asking for forgiveness, and making a true commitment out loud to God that we are turning away from our sin, and obeying His word. Let's do this together!

2. IS THERE ANY REASON WE CAN'T BAPTIZE YOU IN THE NAME OF THE LORD JESUS CHRIST, AND PRAY WITH YOU UNTIL GOD FILLS YOU WITH THE GIFT OF THE HOLY GHOST?

Maybe you have already been baptized a different way, such as in the titles Father, Son, and Holy Ghost. IT IS NOT TOO LATE. People are being re-baptized all over the world the Bible Way, in the name of Jesus Christ! Maybe you were baptized and do not remember what was spoken over you. If that is the case, let's baptize you in the name of Jesus Christ so you can be 100% sure!

NOTES

NOTES

BIBLE STUDY LOG

#	STUDENT NAME	CONTACT INFO	DATE TAUGHT
1			
2			
3			
4			
5			
6			
7			
8			
9			
10			
11			
12			
13			
14			
15			
16			
17			
18			
19			
20			
21			
22			
23			
24			

#	STUDENT NAME	CONTACT INFO	DATE TAUGHT
25			
26			
27			
28			
29			
30			
31			
32			
33			
34			
35			
36			
37			
38			
39			
40			
41			
42			
43			
44			
45			
46			
47			
48			
49			
50			

RESOURCES FROM
TAYLOR FISH

MUSIC: Follow Taylor Fish on Spotify
BOOKS + RESOURCES: Visit linktr.ee/revtaylorfish
INSTAGRAM: @revtaylorfish

To place a wholesale order of *The Simple Salvation Bible Study*,
contact us at: **wholesale@truthbook.co**

Made in the USA
Columbia, SC
24 September 2024

42284381R00015